The Scottish Toast Master

First published in 2007 by

Appletree Press Ltd
The Old Potato Station
14 Howard Street South
Belfast BT7 1AP

Tel: +44 (028) 90 24 30 74
Fax: +44 (028) 90 24 67 56
Email: reception@appletree.ie
Web: www.appletree.ie

A catalogue record for this book is available from the British Library.

The Scottish Toast Master

ISBN: 978 1 84758 009 2

Desk & Marketing Editor: Jean Brown
Copy-editing: Jim Black
Designer: Stuart Wilkinson
Production Manager: Paul McAvoy

9 8 7 6 5 4 3 2 1

AP3416

The Scottish Toast Master

Charles MacLean

Contents

Contents

Introduction

Before humans drank the health of the living, they drank the *minni* of the dead or of the gods. *Minni* is Old Norse and means "love, memory and thought of the absent one" all at the same time. With Christians it became "God's *minni*"; in medieval times there were "*minnying*" or "*mynde*" days, and even today Scots use the verb "*mind*" rather than "remember".

Drinking the health of the living was closely associated with *minnying*. Greeks and Romans drank to one another; Goths pledged each other with *hails* ("health") and Saxons with *waes hael* ("be in health").

It was a Saxon, Margaret "Atheling", great-niece of King Edward the Confessor and wife of the Scottish King Malcolm Canmore, who first introduced the "grace cup" as a means of inducing the restless Scots to remain at table until grace had been said at the end of the meal. Queen Margaret, who arrived in Scotland in about 1069 (after being driven out of England by the Norman Conquest) was

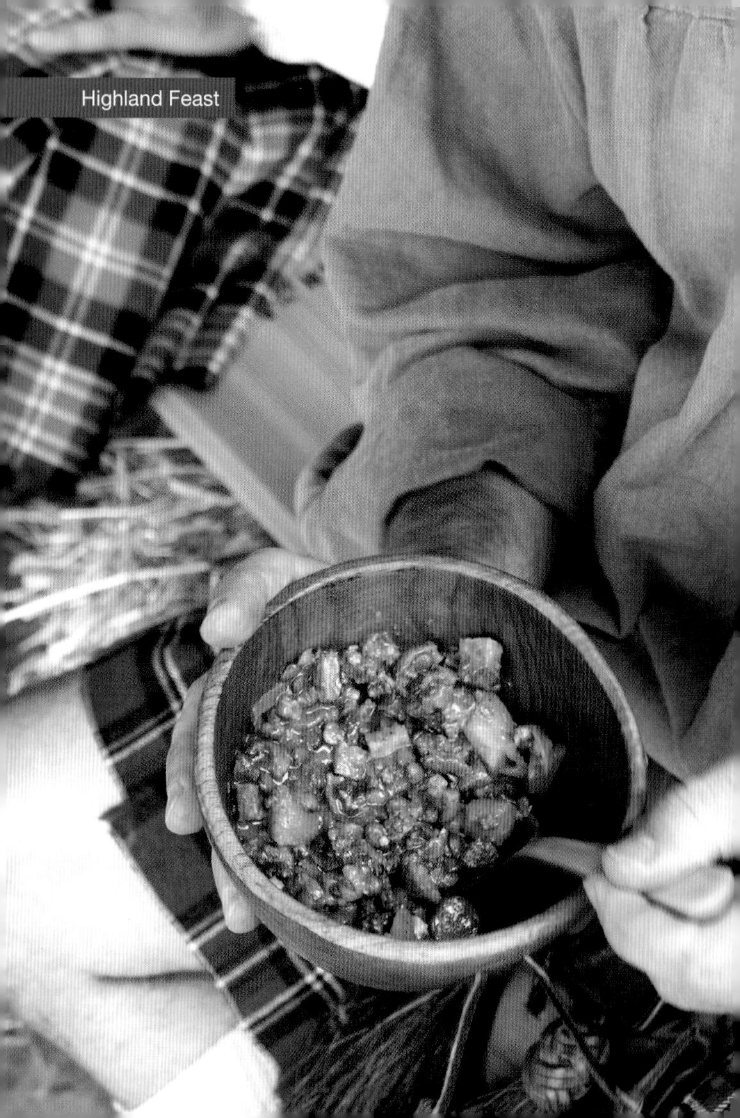

so devout she was canonised. She arranged that a cup of the finest available wine should be passed round, but only after grace had been said.

In this context, "grace" means "giving thanks". The custom of saying grace either before or after a meal was widely practised by the Jews, Greeks and Romans and adopted universally by Christians, who often commenced with the words *Gratias Deo agamus* ("let us give thanks to God"), a formula which originated in monastic refectories.

While on the subject of word origins, the commonest toast of all, "cheers", entered the English language in the thirteenth century via the Anglo-Norman *chere*, meaning "face", and derives from the Latin *cara*. "Face" quickly became a metaphor for the state of the mind behind it, hence "be of good cheer", "be cheerful", "cheers".

The origin of making "toasts" is more obscure. The word derives from the Vulgar Latin *tostare* (to scorch or roast). From Classical times it was common to flavour wine by floating small pieces of toasted bread in it. Sometimes these sippets would be flavoured with spices; at other times the carbon alone would mellow the wine. It is supposed that the drinking of "toasts" derives from the gallantry that "the name of the lady (to whom one was drinking) enhanced the drink more than any toast". This usage first appears in the seventeenth century.

Sir Richard Steele explained the practice of drinking toasts in the *Tatler*, June 4th 1709, recalling an event that had taken place at Bath some thirty years before:

"It happened that on a publick day a celebrated beauty of those times was in the cross bath, and one of the crowd of her admirers took a glass of the water in which the fair one stood, and drank her health to the company. There was in the place a gay fellow, half fuddled, who offered to jump in, and swore, though he liked not the liquor, he would have the toast. He was opposed in his resolution; yet this whim

gave foundation to the present honour which is done to the lady we mention in our liquor, who has ever since been called a toast."

In Scotland, during the eighteenth century, toasting was all the rage – at every level of society. The custom was frequently used as an excuse for intemperate drinking, or as a way of compelling guests to drink. Each time the glasses were filled, someone was called upon to make a toast (or "sentiment" as they were also called). Often the toast-maker would insist that the toast must be emphasised by drinking a "bumper" (i.e. draining the glass). He would then call upon the next to make a toast, or if he had toasted somebody present, they would rise, reply and toast another. Often the rounds of toasts went on for some time: When George IV visited Edinburgh in August 1822, forty-seven toasts were pronounced at the banquet in his honour!

In his *Memorials of My Time*, published in the 1850s, Lord Cockburn, the eminent Scottish judge, remembers:

"After dinner, and before the ladies retired, there generally began what was called 'Rounds' of toasts, when each gentleman named an absent lady, and each lady an absent gentleman, and the persons named were toasted, generally with allusions and jokes about the fitness of the union. And worst of all there were 'Sentiments'. These were short epigrammatic sentences expressive of moral feelings and virtues, and were thought refined and elegant productions...The conceited, the ready or the feckless, hackneyed in the art, had a knack of making new sentiments applicable to passing incidents with great ease. But it was a dreadful oppression on the timid or the awkward."

Elsewhere he recalls:

"Every glass during dinner had to be dedicated to some one. It was thought sottish and rude to take wine without this, as if forsooth there was nobody present worth drinking with. I was present about

1803 when the late Duke of Buccleuch took a glass of sherry by himself at the table of Charles Hope, then Lord Advocate, and this was noticed afterwards as a piece of direct contempt."

"Rounds" often went on until the company fell unconscious beneath the table. Dean Ramsay, in his *Reminiscences of Scottish Life and Character* (1857), recounts an incident which had been told him by Duncan Mackenzie, a celebrated author of the early nineteenth century:

"He had been involved in a regular drinking party. He was keeping as free from the usual excesses as he was able, and as he marked companions around him falling victims to the power of drink, he himself dropped off under the table amongst the slain, as a measure of precaution, and lying there, his attention was called to a small pair of hands working at his throat; on asking what it was, a voice replied, 'Sir, I'm the lad that's to lowse the neck-cloths'

(i.e. to untie the cravats of the guests and prevent apoplexy or suffocation)*".*

And again:

"There had been a carousing party at Castle Grant, many years ago, and as the evening advanced towards morning two Highlanders were in attendance to carry the guests upstairs, it being understood that none could by any other means arrive at their sleeping apartments. One or two of the guests, whether from their abstinence or their superior strength of head, were walking upstairs, and declined the proffered assistance. The attendants were astonished, and indignantly exclaimed, 'Ach, it's sare cheenged times at Castle Grant, when gentlemens can get to bed on their ain feet'!"

Not surprising, then, that the Golden Age for Scottish toasts are the eighteenth and early nineteenth centuries. This little book contains many examples. But toasts are continually being invented, updated, personalised, and it is to be hoped that, as well as being a repository of examples of a curious human activity, *The Scottish Toast Master* might inspire its readers to create their own toasts, in the knowledge that they are continuing a convivial tradition which stretches back at least three hundred years.

The Poet's Graces

These graces were made extempore, and were first published in the *Edinburgh Courant* in August 1789. In more recent times they have become known as "The Poet's Graces".

Before the meal

O Thou who kindly dost provide
For every creature's want!
We bless Thee, God of Nature wide,
For all thy goodness lent.
And, if it please Thee, heavenly Guide,
May never worse be sent;
But, whether granted or denied,
Lord bless us with content.

Robert Burns

Sunset from Holyrood Park looking over the Firth of Forth

After the Meal

O Thou, in whom we live and move,
Who made the sea and shore;
Thy goodness constantly we prove,
And grateful would adore;
And, if it please Thee, Power above!
Still grant us with such store
The friend we trust, the fair we love,
And we desire no more.

Robert Burns

At the Globe Tavern

The Globe Tavern in Tarbolton, Ayrshire, was one of Burns' haunts.

Grace Before Meat

O Lord, when hunger pinches sore,
Do Thou stand us in stead,
And send us, from Thy bounteous store,
A tup – or wether-head!

(*tup* – a young ram; *wether-head* – a sheep's head)

Grace After Meat

Lord Thee we thank, and Thee alone,
For temporal gifts we little merit!
At present we will ask no more:
Let William Hislop bring the spirit.

'A tup - or wether-head!"

O Lord since we have feasted thus,
Which we so little merit,
Let Meg now take the flesh away,
And Jock bring in the spirit.

O Lord, we do Thee humbly thank
For that we little merit:
Now Jean may tak the flesh away,
And Will bring in the spirit.

An early (1801) version of 'Grace After Meat' has "Let William Hislop bring the spirit" as its concluding line – Hislop was the landlord. "Meg" and "Jock" were variations for different occasions.

From: 'There was a Lass, they ca'd her Meg'

A man may drink and no be drunk;
A man may fight and no be slain;
A man may kiss a bonnie lass,
And aye be welcome back again.

Robert Burns

Scotch Drink

Freedom and Whisky gang thegither –
Tak aff your dram!

Robert Burns

Burns was fond of whisky although, at the time he wrote, it was not as generally available in the Lowlands as it is today. This is one of his most quoted "bumper" toasts.

The following preface to Burns' poem *Scotch Drink* was inspired by Proverbs xxxi: 6-7: "Give strong drink to the desperate and wine to the embittered; such men will drink and forget their poverty and remember their trouble no longer". The poem was written during the winter 1785-1786.

Gie him strong drink until he wink,
That's sinking in despair;
An' liquor guid to fire his bluid,
That's prest wi' grief an' care:
There let him bowse, and deep carouse,
Wi' bumpers flowing o'er,
Till he forgets his loves or debts
An' minds his griefs no more.

A Bottle and Friend

Here's a bottle and an honest friend!
What wad ye wish for mair, man?
Wha kens, before his life may end,
What his share may be o' care, man?

Then catch the moments as they fly,
And use them as ye ought, man.
Believe me happiness is shy,
And comes not aye when sought, man!

Robert Burns

(*mair* – more; *wha* – who; *kens* – knows)

This first appears in a MS of 1808. The sentiment was echoed by William Blake in his famous "Gnomic" verse:

'He who bends to himself a Joy
Doth the winged life destroy;
But he who kisses the Joy as it flies
Lives in Eternity's sunrise.'

O Fortuna!

When we're gaun up the hill o' Fortune,
May we ne'er meet a frien' comin' doun!

May puirtith ne'er throw us in the mire,
or gowd in the high saddle

Dean Ramsay

(*puirtith* – poverty; *mire* – mud; *gowd* – gold)

"Fortune" – good and bad – was even more acutely felt by our forefathers than by us today. So it is not surprising that so many toasts were devoted to it. Dean Ramsay (1793-1872), was an Episcopalian clergyman in Edinburgh. In *Reminiscences of Scottish Life and Character* (published in 1858, it went into twenty-one editions during its author's lifetime, and was described by Sydney Smith as "one of the best answers to the charge of want of humour in the Scots") he lists several prosaic examples, including:

May the honest heart ne'er feel distress

May the winds of adversity ne'er blow in your door

An earlier, and monumental, work entitled *A Complete Collection of Scottish Proverbs* (James Kelly M.A.; London, 1721) includes the charming toast:

Better the heid o' the yeomanry than the arse o' the gentry!

Country road in the Scottish Highlands

Here's Tae Us…

Here's tae us –
Wha's like us –
Damn few;
And they're a' deid –
Mair's the pity!

(i.e. 'Here's to us and those like us – there aren't many, and those that were are all dead. More's the pity!')

This "Golden Age" toast is still common today in Scotland. Solidarity amongst topers is another familiar theme of toasting through the ages:

Here's to them that lo'es us, or lends us a lift!

May ye ne'er want a frien' or a dram to gie him

May we be happy and our enemies know it!

Here's to them that like us –
Them that think us swell –
And here's tae them that hate us –
Let's pray for them as well.

– and, of course, the famous (and still current)
Edinburgh toast:

'Lang may yer lum reek –
Wi' ither folks coal!'

(*lum reek* – chimney smoke)

Edinburgh Chimneys

Blackrock cottage, Scotland

A Man's A Man for A' That

Is there for honest poverty
That hings his head, and a' that?
The coward slave, we pass him by –
We dare be poor, for a' that!
For a' that, and a' that.
Our toils obscure and a' that.
The rank is but the guinea's stamp,
The man's the gowd, for a' that.

What though on hamely fare we dine,
Wear hodden grey and a' that?
Gie fools their silks, and knaves their wine –
A man's a man for a' that.
For a' that and a' that.
Their tinsel show, and a' that,
The honest man, though e'er sae poor,
Is king o' men for a' that.

Robert Burns

Health, Wealth and Happiness

Here's health to the sick,
Stilts to the lame,
Claes to the back,
And brose to the wame!

(*claes* – clothes; *brose* – soup, drink; *wame* – stomach)

Variations include:

May ye aye be happy,
And ne'er drink from a toom cappie!

(*toom cappie* – empty bowl)

The ingle-neuk, wi'routh o' bannocks and bairns

(i.e. The corner by the fire, with plenty of oat-cakes and children)

May we a' be canty and cosy,
And ilk hae a wife in his bosy!

(*canty* – lively; *ilk* – each; *bosy* – bosom)

Or simply:

Thumping luck and fat weans!

(*weans* – children)

Scottish hospitality

There's Nae Luck Aboot the Hoose...

May the best ye've ever seen
Be the worst ye'll ever see;
May a moose ne'er leave yer girnal
Wi' a tear drap in his ee.
May ye aye keep hale and he'erty
Till ye're auld enough tae dee,
May ye aye be juist as happy
As I wish ye aye tae be.

(*moose* – mouse; *girnal* – meal chest)

This toast might be termed "transitional". The first two lines are traditional, and often quoted (by Dean Ramsay among others), but this full version has the sentimentality of the nineteenth-century music hall.

Hi-Jinks

Good wine, a friend, or being dry –
Or lest you should be bye and bye –
Or any other reason why.

Allan Ramsay

How to play Hi-jinks

"Hi-jinks. A drunken game, or new project to drink and be rich" begins the distinguished poet Allan Ramsay (1686-1758) in describing this popular Scottish pastime.

1. Once the glass is filled to the brim, one of the company takes a pair of dice (or more if you're feeling brave!), cries "Hi-jinks" and rolls them.

2. The number cast indicates who must drink the bumper, or pay a forfeit if he declines (in which case he cries "Hi-jinks" and throws again, to choose another).

Hi-jinks–'A rare project this'

3. If he chooses to drink he takes whatever is in the kitty, but only if he fulfills the procedure exactly: drinks the bumper; sweeps up the money; fills the glass to the brim; cries "Hi-jinks"; and counts the numbers of the dice correctly.

Ramsay concludes: "A rare project this, and no bubble I can assure you: for a covetous fellow may save money, and get himself as drunk as he can desire in less than an hour's time".

The Bon Accord

Blythe to meet,
Wae to part,
Blythe to meet aince mair.

(i.e. Happy to meet, sorrowful to part, happy to meet once more)

Guid nicht to ye, and tak yer nappie:
A willie-waught's a guid nicht-cappie!

(i.e. Good night to you, and drink up your ale – A friendly drink's a good night-cap)

Blythe, blythe aroun' the nappie
Let us join in social glee:
While we're here we'll hae a drappie –
Scotia's sons have aye been free!

(*nappie* – strong ale; *aye* – always)

These toasts come from the North-east of Scotland. The first is known as "The Bon-Accord Toast". *Bon Accord* is the motto of the City of Aberdeen, and originated in 1308, when the citizens of the town rose up one night in a sudden and secret insurrection, massacred the (English) garrison in the castle and seized the town for Robert the Bruce. "Bon-Accord" was the watchword they adopted during the operation.

Statue of Robert the Bruce

The Great Toast

Suas i, suas i;
Seas i, seas i;
A'nall i, a'nall i;
A'null i, a'null i.
Na h'uile la gu math diut, mo charaid.
Sguab as i!
Agus cha n'ol neach eile as a ghloine so gu
brath!

Translation:

Up with it, up with it;
Down with it, down with it;
Over to you; over to you
Over to me; over to me.
May all your days be good, my friend.
Drink it up!
And let no one ever drink from this glass
again!

This toast is properly drunk standing on a
chair, with one foot on the table. The glass is
raised and lowered, brought in and out, with

each line, drained on the words *Sguab as i*, and smashed at the end.

A charming variant is:

Neither above you,
Nor below you –
Always with you

Scotland - 'Always with you'

The Toast Master's Companion

The Toastmaster's Companion was published in Stirling in 1822 – the year George IV visited Edinburgh – and provides a useful insight into the topics that interested the drinking classes at that time.

May opinion never float on the waves of ignorance

May we look forward with pleasure, and backwards without remorse

May we never crack a joke to break a reputation

May we never suffer for principles we do not hold

To the man that feels for sorrows not his own

Great men honest, and honest men great

Edinburgh Skyline

May we live to learn and learn to live well

May we live in pleasure and die out of debt

A head to earn and a heart to spend

Health of body, peace of mind, a clean shirt and a guinea

Well Met!

Here's our noble sel's, weel met the day!

Robert Fergusson

The poet Robert Fergusson (1750–1774) was born in Edinburgh, of humble parents (his father was a draper's clerk) but soon moved to Dundee, where he won a scholarship to the Grammar School and later to the University

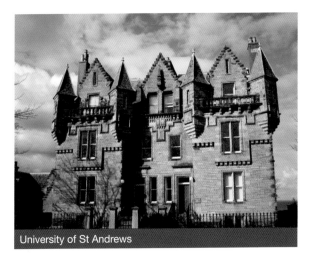

University of St Andrews

of St Andrews. Here he distinguished himself both as a student of science and for his high-spirited, hard-living and impulsive character.

Fergusson was greatly admired by Robert Burns. In one poem he celebrates the "Daft Days" between Christmas and the first Monday of the New Year:

Let mirth abound, let social cheer
Invest the dawning of the year;
Let blithesome innocence appear
To crown our joy,
Nor envy wi' sarcastic sneer
Our bliss destroy
And thou, great god of Aqua Vitae!
Wha sways the empire of this city,
Where fou we're sometimes capernoity,
Be thou prepar'd
To hedge us frae that black banditti,
The City-Guard.

In this verse from 'The King's Birth-Day in Edinburgh' Fergusson's admiration for whisky is clear:

I sing the day sae aften sung,
Wi' which our lugs hae yearly rung,
In whase loud praise the Muse has dung
A' kind o' print;
But wow! the limmer's fairly flung;
There's naething in't.
I'm fain to think the joys the same
In London town as here at hame,
Whare fock of ilka age and name,
Baith blind and cripple,
Forgather aft, O fy for shame!
To drink and tipple.
O Muse, be kind, and dinna fash us
To flee awa' beyont Parnassus,
Nor seek for Helicon to wash us,
That heath'nish spring;
Wi' Highland whisky scour our hawses,
And gar us sing.
Begin then, dame, ye've drunk your fill,
You wouldna hae the tither gill?

(*lugs* – ears, *dung* – used, subdued; *limmer* – low woman; *fou* – drunk; *capernoity* – peevish, irritable; *dinna fash us* – don't vex us, make us angry; *scour our hawses* – clean out our throats; *gar* – make)

Toasts to Love

May those who love truly be always believed,
And those who deceive us be always deceived.

Here's to the men of all classes,
Who through lasses and glasses
Will make themselves asses!

I drink to the health of another,
And the other I drink to is he –
In the hope that he drinks to another,
And the other he drinks to is me.

Wit, or what passed for it in intoxicated company, was what the toast-makers of the eighteenth century mainly sought to display. The Scottish repertoire is full of verbal tricks to confuse the tipsy and make the toaster seem wise. Typical examples are:

A guid wife and health: a man's best wealth!

A bagpiper at Gretna Green

May we never want a friend to cheer us, or a bottle to cheer him!

Hard drinking of the kind that went on during The Enlightenment was rarely enjoyed by women. Predictably, therefore, sex, love and marriage were always popular topics – with toasts such as:

The dignity of the Fair Sex.

Success to the lover and joy to the beloved.

Days of peace and nights of pleasure!

Scotland Yet

Gae bring my guid auld harp aince mair;
Gae bring it free and fast,
For I maun sing anither sang
Ere a' my glee be past:
And trow ye as I sing, my lads,
The burthen o't shall be –
Auld Scotland's howes and Scotland's knowes,
And Scotland's hills for me!

I'll drink a cup to Scotland yet,
Wi' a' the honours three!

The heath waves wild upon her hill
And foaming through the fells,
Her fountains sing of freedom still,
As they dash down the dells;
For weel I loe the land, my lads,
That's girded by the sea –
Then Scotland's vales, and Scotland's dales,
And Scotland's hills for me;

The Wallace Monument

I'll drink a cup to Scotland yet,
Wi' a' the honours three!

The thistle wags upon the fields
Where Wallace bore his blade,
That gave her foe-men's dearest bluid
To dye her auld grey plaid:
And, looking to the lift my lads,
He sang in doughty glee –
"Auld Scotland's right, and Scotland's might,
And Scotland's hills for me!"

Then drink a cup to Scotland yet,
Wi' a' the honours three!

(*gae* – go; *aince* – once; *maun* – must; *glee* – joy; *trow* – know, *feel* sure about; *howes and knowes* – hollows and knolls; *Wallace* – Sir William Wallace, the "Father of Scottish nationhood")

A Toast to Whisky

John Barleycorn was a hero bold,
Of noble enterprise;
For if you do but taste his blood,
'Twill make your courage rise.

'Twill make a man forget his woe;
'Twill heighten all his joy;
'Twill make the widow's heart to sing,
Tho' the tear were in her eye.

Then let us toast John Barleycorn,
Each man a glass in hand;
And may his great posterity
Ne'er fail in old Scotland!

Robert Burns

Whisky has been drunk in Scotland since time immemorial: a strong tradition holds that its manufacture was introduced from Ireland, and that it was brought to Ireland by St Patrick, who came from what is now southern Scotland.

A distillation room at a distillery

The earliest documentary reference to whisky appears in the Scottish Exchequer Rolls for 1494 – "eight bolls of malt to Friar John Cor wherewith to make aquavitae".

The name "whisky" derives from the Gaelic for *aquavitae – uisge beatha*: the Water of Life – but the term was not in general use in the Lowlands until the eighteenth century.

By the 1570s so much whisky was being produced for domestic consumption that there was a shortage of grain for making bread and bannocks but, until the eighteenth century, Scotland's "national" drinks were claret (for those who could afford it) and home-brewed ale, known as "two-penny ale" (or "tipenny").

Robert Burns refers to this in *Tam o'Shanter* (1790):

Inspiring, bold John Barleycorn,
What dangers thou canst make us scorn!
Wi' tipenny, we fear nae evil:
Wi' usquebae, we'll face the devil!

Tartan Heroes

Here's to the heath, the hill and the heather,
The bonnet, the plaid, the kilt and the feather!

Here's to the heroes that Scotland can boast,
May their names never dee –
That's the Heilan' Man's toast!

(*dee* – die)

Let's drink a drop o' barley bree,
Though moon and stars should blink thegither:
To each leaf lad wi' kilted knee,
And bonnie lass amang the heather.

(*bree* – drink, liquor)

Cloying sentimentality and tartan absurdity became identified with Scotland during the late nineteenth century, promulgated by music hall artists such as Harry Lauder. These toasts are worthy only of picture postcards illustrated with thistles and Scottie dogs.

Such toasts do have provenance, however. An earlier, Gaelic, version runs:

Tir nam beann, nan gleann, nan gaisach!

(i.e. To the land of the bens, the glens and the heroes!)

'Here's to the Heroes!'

The Tartan

Here's to it.

The fighting sheen o' it;
The yellow, the green o' it;
The black, the red o' it;
Every thread o' it.
The fair have sighed for it;
The brave have died for it;
Foemen sought for it;
Heroes faught for it;
Honour the name o' it;
Drink to the fame o' it –
THE TARTAN.

This is a further example of Victorian sentimentality, wrong in every particular.

Tartan cloth has been worn by Gaels since time immemorial – there is a fragment of checked cloth in the Royal Scottish Museum, known as the "Falkirk Tartan", which dates from the third century AD – but the pattern of the cloth was not originally an expression of identity or membership of a clan. Plaids and bolts of cloth were looted during clan raids, and the smokey atmosphere that most clansfolk lived in will have ensured that their tartan's original colours became kippered. Tartan only became part of the definition of clanship after 1822.

Regimental Toasts

From the Royal Scots

Slainte mhath, h-uile latha, na chi 'snach fhaic. Slainte!

(i.e. Good health, every day, whether I see you or not. Health!)

From the Scots Guards

Deoch slainte ne bhan Righ

i.e. God's health to the Queen

After he has played his *piobroch* at a regimental dinner, the Pipe Major receives a *quaich* (Gaelic for cup; a silver bowl, with a small handle on either side) of whisky from the Commanding Officer. He pronounces the regimental toast, drains the *quaich*, finishes with "*Slainte*", salutes and marches out.

Decorative quaich

For St Andrew's Night

Gentlemen, let us drink in solemn silence to the pious memory of our patron saint, St Andrew

Most Scottish regiments celebrate St Andrew's Night with a dinner. After the meal, the regimental *quaich* is carried round by the Colour Sergeant and presented to each officer in turn. The officer rises to receive the *quaich*, as do those on his either side (to protect him). He drinks, kisses the bottom of the *quaich* and passes it back to the Colour Sergeant, who continues round the table.

Here's Looking at You...

Here's to me and here's to you,
And if in the world
There was just us two –
And I could promise that nobody knew –
Would you?

This is a modern toast, but it echoes the original tradition of "toasting", which honoured the fair sex, often with innuendo.

Examples from the Scottish repertoire are numerous, some of them unprintable:

Virtuous desires and those desires gratified!

The maiden's blush, and a virgin of fifteen!

Love and opportunity!

Days of ease and nights of pleasure!

Old wine and young women!

Eilean Donan - Scotland's most romantic castle?

Undoubtedly the most famous variation on this theme was Humphrey Bogart's toast in *Casablanca*:

Here's looking at you, kid.

Another touching variation on this is the (possibly Irish) Gaelic toast:

I look towards you,
And I gently smells your breath

Jock Tamson's Bairns

Scots are all "Jock Tamson's Bairns" whatever their rank or degree, and by implication the expression embraces the people of the entire Earth.

The phrase has been in common use in Scotland since at least the early nineteenth century – one traveller in the West (1827) recorded: "when a company are (sic) sitting together, and a neighbour drops in, it is usual to welcome him thus: 'Come awa, we're a' John Tamson's bairns'." Another recorded (1847) the familiar welcome: "Nae ceremony, we're a' Jock Tamson's bairns here".

The derivation of the term is obscure, although, interestingly, "Jock Tamson" was once a jocular name for whisky. The original meaning probably embraced a group united by common sentiment or purpose, but the contemporary meaning was made plain by Kate Rennie Archer, the poet, in 1934:

We're a' Jock Tamson's bairnies.
An' Jock Tamson? Weel – he's God.

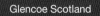
Glencoe Scotland

A Gaelic Blessing

May the hill rise behind you,
And may the mountain be always over the crest;
And may the God that you believe in
Hold you in the palm of his hand.

There are several charming variations of this toast in Ireland as well as Scotland, such as:

May the Lord keep you in his hand,
And never close his fist too tight on you.

and

May the road rise to meet you;
May the wind be always at your back,
The sun shine warm upon your face,
The rain fall soft upon your fields.
And until we meet again,
May God hold you in the hollow of his hand.

A church in the West Highands of Scotland.
It was also used in the movie *Local Hero*

Scottish Graces

Be with me, o God, at the breaking of bread,
Be with me, o God, when I have fed;
Naught come to my body my soul to pain
Naught able my contrite soul to stain.

From the Gaelic

Without Thy sunshine and Thy rain,
We would not have Thy golden grain.
Without Thy love we'd not be fed:
We thank Thee for our daily bread.

From the Gaelic

Burns Statue, Dumfries

Robert Burns –
The Toast of Scotland

Robert Burns' life-story is a fascinating one and too long to cover in this brief text. It is a richly interesting human story, and such was the magnetism of Burns' personality that it still remains powerful after two centuries. He was born during a stormy night in Alloway, Ayrshire on 25th January 1759. He was the first child of a struggling tenant farmer William Burnes (the 'e' was later dropped) and his wife Agnes. He spent much of his childhood working on the farm and the legacy of hard childhood work and indeed throughout his life weakened his health and contributed to the rheumatic fever which would later lead to his death.

As a child 'Robin' was clever but the poverty of his family meant that he was unable to escape a lifetime of drudgery on the farm. There was simply no money to spare but by the age of fifteen, even if his future prospects looked grim, he could escape into the world of poetry and he had already written the first of his love poems. Love and poetry would run together for him for the rest of his life. As we have seen from just the small sample of his verse quoted in this guide he was undoubtably the author of some of the best-known and loved poems in literature.

Robert Burns was just thirty-seven when he died and he was buried on 26th July 1796 in Dumfries on the day that his wife gave birth to their ninth child. The people of Dumfries and very soon afterwards the people of Scotland realised that they had lost someone incomparable. As is often the case, it was easier to recognise his worth after his death, than it had been when he was alive. In life even a genius such as Burns had his share of human frailties and pressures. In death, only the genius and the works it produced remains and as a result 'The Immortal Memory" of Burns is celebrated at Burns Night Suppers thoughout Scotland.

The first Burns Night is believed to have been held in July 1801 on the fifth anniversary of his death, and was held by a group of his friends and acquaintances.

Later the date would change to the happier anniversary date of his birthday – 25th January. Nowadays Burns Suppers tend to be held on any occasion with a Scottish link, such as St Andrew's Day on 30th November, a reunion of Scots at home or abroad, or at Hogmanay. It is an excuse for the Scots and those of Scottish descent to gather with friends, enjoy a meal and simply revel in the pride of being Scottish. It is hard to say what Burns himself would have thought of it. He would have enjoyed it as an excuse to gather with friends, but he would have probably have laughed at the 'ceremony' of it all.

How to Throw a Burns' Night Party

There is no one hard and fast rule here. Include as little or as much of the ceremony as you wish: it will be just as much fun. It's something everyone can enjoy and the 'ceremony' of the event is all part of the fun. The chief ingredients are: a haggis, neeps, tatties, good friends and fun!

Piping in of the Guests
If the event is large the audience will stand and clap in time to the music as the special guests and speakers enter in single file and take their seats.

The Chairman's Welcome
The Chairman will welcome everyone and introduce the guest speakers and entertainers.

Selkirk Grace
This traditional prayer of thanks to start the evening. (For full text see page 82).

The Piping in of the Haggis

The guests are asked to stand up to receive the guest of honour – the haggis. The piper enters, leading a small procession consisting of the chef, carrying the haggis on a platter, the person who will 'address the haggis', and someone carrying a tray with 'tots' of whiskey to toast the haggis. The procession should march in single file and the guests clap in time to the music. If you don't have your own piper, everyone can still clap in time to a CD of Scottish music. Any song by Burns will be fine. Music stops as the top table is reached and the haggis is set down in view of everyone.

Address to the Haggis

The appointed speaker should recite 'The Address to the Haggis' (see page 84) with as much feeling and gusto as they can muster. This is all part of the entertainment. The reciter should take his knife (a sgian dhu is even better if you have one) and dramatically cut into the haggis during the line:

'An' cut you up with ready slight'.

'…trenching its gushing entrails',
he should dig into the haggis in similiar dramatic fashion. The speaker should present aloft the platter of haggis during the final line, taking great care not to drop it or spill it over himself or the other guests. The guests should applaud again.

Toast to the Haggis
The speaker should ask everyone to raise their glass to 'The Haggis'. The procession proceeds out to the kitchen to serve the meal, to music and the clapping of the audience.

The Meal
A Burns Supper is traditionally a haggis served with 'bashit neeps' (mashed turnip/swede) and 'champit tatties' (mashed potatoes). Vegetable-based versions of haggis are available so vegetarians can join in the fun. If you wish you can serve starters of Cock-a-Leekie soup or Scotch Broth. Suitable desserts can include Clootie Dumpling (a fruit dumpling wrapped, then tied in a cloth to preserve its shape during boiling). Or you

may prefer a cheeseboard with Scottish cheeses and oatcakes. Many people just have the main course by itself.

Entertainment
This is a good way for your guests to get involved and they could either recite a poem by Burns, such as 'A Man's A Man For A' That' or even sing one of Burns' songs. Further entertainment can be planned between each of the speeches if you desire.

The Immortal Memory
After the meal the speaker should make a speech on the life of Robert Burns. He should tell the audience about his contribution to literature, his principles, his kindly character and his national pride. The speech should be in keeping with the spirit of the evening and the character of Burns himself – full of bon-homie, passion and humour. The speech should conclude with an invitation to raise your glass to 'The Immortal Memory of Robert Burns'. What you drink is up to you. Some people may not wish to make a speech: if not, just the Toast itself is fine.

Toasts to the Lassies
One of the male guests should make a speech about women and particularly those in Burns' life. It should be funny but end on a positive note and the men should raise their glasses: 'To the Lassies'.

The Lassies Reply
One of the Lassies makes her own speech in 'thanks', referring to the women in Burns' life and the men in their own lives!

The Vote of Thanks
The Chairman should thank all the speechmakers, piper, guests and most importantly the chef/cook for their contribution to the event.

Auld Lang Syne
At the conclusion of the event the speaker should ask everyone to stand and sing the song most often associated with Burns, 'Auld Lang Syne' (see page 89). Traditionally sung at Hogmanay, the song is a fun way to conclude the festivities of any Burns Night.

The Selkirk Grace

Some hae meat, and canna eat,
And some wad eat that want it;
But we hae meat, and we can eat –
And sae the Lord be thankit.

Robert Burns

This grace takes its name from a person, Dunbar Douglas, 4th Earl of Selkirk, rather than the town in the Scottish Borders. In fact, Robert Burns only visited Selkirk once. He was touring with a companion, and arrived at Selkirk on Sunday 13th May 1787. It was raining hard, so they took shelter in Veitch's Inn, where the local doctor and two friends were sitting by the fire. The innkeeper asked if the strangers could join them, but the doctor refused, on the grounds that 'they did not look like gentlemen'.

Three days later, Dr Clarkson learned who the stranger was: a contemporary, James Hogg, wrote that "his refusal [to allow them to join him] hangs about the doctor's heart

like a dead weight to this day, and will do
'til the day of his death, for the bard had no
more enthusiastic an admirer".

The grace itself was probably first delivered
at the Heid Inn in Kirkcudbright High Street,
in the presence of Lord Selkirk, in July 1794
(the inn is now named the Selkirk Arms).
It is also possible that this, Burns' most
famous toast, was traditional, and not in fact
composed by him after all. He certainly never
wrote it down.

Address to a Haggis

Surprisingly, since the haggis is such a focal point of a Burns Supper, it was not well known to Robert Burns.

When he was invited to attend an annual harvest supper in 1785 at which a sheep's haggis was traditionally eaten, he wrote the poem in advance: "Everyone thought the grace was extempore, but the Poet himself told them he came prepared for the Haggis but not for the (large) company present" (Grierson).

The entire poem is given here but the first and last of verses are probably the best known and most widely recited.

Fair fa' your honest, sonsie face,
Great chieftain o' the pudding-race!
Aboon them a' yet tak your place,
Painch, tripe, or thairm:
Weel are ye wordy o'a grace
As lang's my arm.

The groaning trencher there ye fill,
Your hurdies like a distant hill,
Your pin was help to mend a mill
In time o'need,
While thro' your pores the dews distil
Like amber bead.

His knife see rustic Labour dight,
An' cut you up wi' ready slight,
Trenching your gushing entrails bright,
Like ony ditch;
And then, O what a glorious sight,
Warm-reekin', rich!

Then, horn for horn, they stretch an' strive:
Deil tak the hindmost! on they drive,
Till a' their weel-swall'd kytes belyve
Are bent like drums;
Then auld Guidman, maist like to rive,
Bethankit! hums.

Is there that owre his French ragout
Or olio that wad staw a sow,
Or fricassee wad make her spew
Wi' perfect sconner,
Looks down wi' sneering, scornfu' view
On sic a dinner?

Poor devil! see him owre his trash,
As feckles as wither'd rash,
His spindle shank, a guid whip-lash;
His nieve a nit;
Thro' blody flood or field to dash,
O how unfit!

But mark the Rustic, haggis-fed,
The trembling earth resounds his tread.
Clap in his walie nieve a blade,
He'll mak it whissle;
An' legs an' arms, an' hands will sned,
Like taps o' trissle.

Ye Pow'rs, wha mak mankind your care,
And dish them out their bill o' fare,
Auld Scotland wants nae skinking ware
That jaups in luggies;
But, if ye wish her gratefu' pray'r
Gie her a haggis!

Robert Burns

(*Fair fa'* – 'may good befall'; *sonsie* – comely, jolly; *aboon* – above; *painch* – paunch, stomach; *thairm* – intestines; *wordy* – worthy; *skinking ware* – slops, thin liquid stuff; *that joups in luggies* – slops around in pails (or two-handed bowls))

Hogmanay in Edinburgh

Auld Lang Syne

Burns did not write the song itself that is perhaps most often associated with him but he did write the poem on which the song was based. Traditionally sung at Hogmanay or a Burns Supper the song is also a popular way to conclude any social occasion in Scotland, such as ceilidhs etc.

Everyone forms a great circle, facing in, crossing their arms with their right hand linking the left hand of their neighbour and vice versa. When everyone has finished singing the song they rush into the middle of the circle still holding hands. When everyone has returned to their starting point they should turn under their arms so that the complete circle now faces out.

Verse 1
Should auld acquaintance be forgot,
And never brought to mind?
Should auld acquaintance be forgot,
And auld lang syne!

Hogmanay Fireworks in Edinburgh

Chorus
For auld lang syne, my dear,
For auld lang syne.
We'll tak a cup o' kindness yet,
For auld lang syne.

Verse 2
And surely ye'll be your pint stowp!
And surely I'll be mine!
And we'll tak a cup o'kindness yet,
For auld lang syne.

Chorus
For auld lang syne, my dear,
For auld lang syne.
We'll tak a cup o' kindness yet,
For auld lang syne.

Verse 3
We twa hae run about the braes,
And pou'd the gowans fine;
But we've wander'd mony a weary fit,
Sin' auld lang syne.

Chorus
For auld lang syne, my dear,
For auld lang syne.
We'll tak a cup o' kindness yet,
For auld lang syne.

Verse 4
We twa hae paidl'd in the burn,
Frae morning sun till dine;
But seas between us braid hae roar'd
Sin' auld lang syne.

Chorus
For auld lang syne, my dear,
For auld lang syne.
We'll tak a cup o' kindness yet,
For auld lang syne.

Verse 5
And there's a hand, my trusty fere!
And gie's a hand o' thine!
And we'll tak a right gude-willie waught,
For auld lang syne.

Chorus
For auld lang syne, my dear,
For auld lang syne.
We'll tak a cup o' kindness yet,
For auld lang syne.

Acknowledgements

The publisher would like to thank the following for permission to reproduce work in copyright:

© istockphoto.com / Andy Green (p4)
© istockphoto.com / Robert Kyllo (p8)
© istockphoto.com / George Clerk (p17)
© istockphoto.com / Andy Twaddle (p20)
© istockphoto.com / inhauscreative (p22)
© John Murphy (p24)
© istockphoto.com / Jamie Farrant (p27)
© istockphoto.com / Ludger Vorfeld (p29)
© istockphoto.com / Mike Bentley (p30)
© istockphoto.com / Linda Macpherson (p33)
© istockphoto.com / Janeen Wassink (p34)
© istockphoto.com / Mark Smith (p36)
© istockphoto.com / Ewan Loughlin (p39)
© istockphoto.com / Duncan Walker (p41)
© istockphoto.com / texasmary (p43)
© istockphoto.com / Stephen Finn (p45)
© istockphoto.com / Andrew Wood (p49)
© istockphoto.com / BMPix (p52)
© istockphoto.com / Mike Bentley (p55)
© istockphoto.com / Mark Atkins (p58)
© istockphoto.com / Allan Munsie (p62)
© istockphoto.com / Jeremy Voisey (p65)
© istockphoto.com / Francisco Orellana (p68)
© istockphoto.com / Jeroen Kloppenburg (p70)
© istockphoto.com / Steve Baxter (p72)
© Tracey Paterson (p76)
© istockphoto.com / Jethro Collins (p88)
© istockphoto.com / David Lochhead (p90)
© istockphoto.com / Tiffany Ring (p94)